C A N A D A

CANADA

LANDSCAPE *of* DREAMS

Photography by

ROBERTA BONDAR

Edited by

CHRISTINE YANKOU

DOUGLAS & McINTYRE
VANCOUVER/TORONTO

Douglas & McIntyre Ltd.
2323 Quebec Street, Suite 201
Vancouver, British Columbia
V5T 4S7
www.douglas-mcintyre.com

LIBRARY AND ARCHIVES CANADA CATALOGUING IN PUBLICATION
Bondar, Roberta Lynn
  Canada: landscape of dreams

  ISBN-13: 978-1-55054-958-4 (bound)   ISBN-10: 1-55054-958-8 (bound)
  ISBN-13: 978-1-55365-182-6 (pbk.)   ISBN-10: 1-55365-182-0 (pbk.)

  1. Landscape photography—Canada. 2. Canada—Pictorial works.
I. Yankou, Christine. II. Title
FC59.B66 2002   779.'3671'092   C2002-910946-9

Design by Val Speidel
Cover photographs by Roberta Bondar
Front cover: Waterton Lakes National Park, Alberta
Back cover: Prince Edward Island National Park, PEI
Printed and bound in Canada by Friesens
Printed on acid-free paper ∞

The quote on page 27 is from Interlunar, copyright © Margaret Atwood, 1984. Used by permission of the author.

The quote on page 57 is from The Fourth Morningside Papers by Peter Gzowski. Used by permission, McClelland & Stewart Ltd. The Canadian Publishers.

We gratefully acknowledge the financial support of the Canada Council for the Arts, the British Columbia Arts Council, the Province of British Columbia through the Book Publishing Tax Credit, and the Government of Canada through the Book Publishing Industry Development Program (BPIDP) for our publishing activities.

LIST OF ILLUSTRATIONS

As a child, I LONGED TO SOAR INTO SPACE, REACHING OUT TO ADVENTURE WITH MY BODY

as well as my imagination. When, as an astronaut, I floated high above Earth in the space shuttle *Discovery*,

my personal vision wrapped around the planet I could no longer touch. I anticipated the exciting moment

when the satisfaction of achieving one goal could slide into defining the next one. I was also changing

perspective.

Away from civilization, my mind was flooded with thoughts that blocked out any consideration

of sleep. The first realization was that I would return to Earth, drawn back by the gravitational pull of the

planet on the shuttle rather than on human willpower. The second was more profound. I realized that,

in my lifetime, I would not leave Earth's orbit. Yet it was the third thought that filled me with butterflies

that seemed to gather, gently flexing their space wings on the walls of my stomach. I understood that the

planet I was returning to, that I had circled for days, was a place about which I knew little.

Although I have ambitions of exploring the whole of the Earth's surface since my return, the planet

is simply too big. To keep the balance between my need to discover and this reality, I have chosen to create themes in my photography. My extensive scientific background shapes the way that I see things and my photographs attempt to communicate the intriguing complexity of both physical and life sciences in the natural world. My challenge is to capture these superb, finely tuned life systems in a way that appeals to the human eye. This does not mean creating landscapes manipulated by humans, but rather identifying and recording on film what exists naturally, and that is real and beautiful to me.

Still "camera in hand" as Ann Thomas, curator of the Photographs Collection at the National Gallery of Canada, uniquely described, I look to my photography to express a personal vision: to capture fleeting moments in time that add value and meaning to my life experience. Canadians are blessed with water, trees, colour, light and texture. Outside of our self-constructed complex social environment we are rich in natural resources that give insight into creation by forces even more complex than any designed by humans. Our curiosity finds adventure there, even an exploration of the meaning of life itself.

One does not have to go into space to be influenced by, or stand in awe of, the natural world. True, space travel jolts us to the reality that nothing else is currently within the touch of a human hand beyond Earth. Living on Earth, however, allows us to interact with the natural world. In a country as vast as Canada, many of us are affected by this land early in life, others later and some throughout our lives. Our experiences with nature may have molded a career path, produced a life-changing moment or even provided a safe haven. Some of us have more than one identity to the natural world.

In my previous book, *Passionate Vision: Discovering Canada's National Parks*, I used quotations about

the natural world to add a reflective mood to a collection of large- and medium-format photographs that I had taken of Canada's preserved lands before the end of the last millennium. This time, I wanted to compare my vision of Canada's natural environment with images captured in the hearts and minds of highly respected Canadians. Not necessarily all of them are known first for their written expressions, but these busy people believe in the land and the importance of it in their lives. From their words I hoped to learn three things: What do they respect and cherish about Canada? What values does the landscape of Canada hold for them? What can we learn about being Canadian?

Each contributor reflected on something personal and meaningful about the natural world we call Canada: a favorite season, a childhood memory, a special attachment to rocks, trees or water. They were free to contribute in poetry or prose, and the results are thoughtful, thought provoking and above all, passionate. These are statements that highlight what's special about our part of the planet.

Selecting the photographs for this book held an element of discovery too. I didn't know what the contributors were going to write, and they didn't know what image I would pair with their words. So it was very exciting when the colour and shapes that appeared on my light table complemented the words from other Canadians. These photographs echo the passion and depth of attachment that the contributors feel to the natural world within Canada. Certain themes emerged. Some photographs speak to the richness of water, others to the density and diversity of terrestrial life. Still others reveal places seldom glimpsed.

Canada, with all its natural beauty and the strength of its people, will continue to evolve into lifetimes beyond our own. We seek solace in the knowledge that the land is strong and eternal. Within the pages of this book, there are photographs of this country that may evoke in you an emotion, a memory or a desire to explore. There are words that express personal views by other Canadians who are not embarrassed to reflect publicly on the interest in and love they have for Canada. I believe that there is something for everyone in this vast land to refresh both body and soul. Where else can we find heaven on Earth?

On the north shore OF THE BIG LAKE, SUPERIOR, EVERY SEASON
brings a richness of light and life and a treasure of sounds and fragrances
that are unique to the Canadian Shield.

From space, I was mesmerized by the lake's expanse, but I longed for
spring smells rising from the earth, granite warmed by the summer sun, crisp
red maple leaves tipped with fall frost, and giant snowflakes drifting lazily
Earthward to blanket the winter landscape.

My space wings could never glide with the loons along the lake's
sandy beach or skim across the glassy, calm blue water. I floated in a world filled
with ever-present humanmade sounds while on Earth, beyond my glass-bottomed
spaceship, there was birdsong that I could not hear.

Roberta Bondar OC

SCIENTIST, PHYSICIAN, ASTRONAUT, PHOTOGRAPHER

There is an obscure myth THAT THE NAME "CANADA" COMES FROM THE

Portuguese words: *ca nao ha nada*, or more simplified *ca nada*, which means "there's nothing."

As the story goes, when the Portuguese cod fishermen first came to the coast of Newfoundland,

they inscribed these words on a rock for future fishing boats to see. Perhaps if they had seen

what lay behind the giant rocks, they would have written *ca nao ha nada mais lindo*, which means

"there's nothing more beautiful."

Bryan Adams OC

MUSICIAN

When I conjure EMOTIONALLY EVOCATIVE IMAGES OF CANADA,

I am transported back to my youth in Bruce County, Ontario, where

everything natural was wonderful: the Saugeen River in the summer where

I learned to swim, the six-foot high snowdrifts in winter where my brother

and I made our first forts. Cities are where I became and remain an adult.

Only when I am alone in nature do I once again see through the eyes

of a child: in the observation car on a train making its way through the

Yellowhead Pass during a winter storm or in the cockpit of a 747

spotting icebergs flowing southward in spring off the Labrador coast.

In this context, my urban Canada is fragile and ephemeral. The natural

Canada of my youth is pure, white, powerful and eternal.

Michael Adams AUTHOR; CO-FOUNDER, ENVIRONICS RESEARCH

SOULFUL DALLIANCE

Seasons slither, dance ONE INTO THE OTHER,

spirits of the past move about claiming the air that is filled

with the scent of change, 1 day, 1 year, 100 years or 1000

years you will always be our place of soulful dalliance.

Susan Aglukark SINGER/SONGWRITER

There is a small arm of a treacherous river near my house. IT IS NOT FORBIDDEN,

but it is private. We walk on the too thin ice. I put my small hand under a rock in the water

and pull out a large frog, legs first, awkward, breech.

When I first heard that someone young had died, I thought of her in the river.

I cannot think of people who are not in places.

This land speaks to us because it carries, forever, a reflection of our humanity.

The Hon. Louise Arbour JUSTICE, SUPREME COURT OF CANADA

Beautiful spring BRINGS SUNLIGHT IN MAY, when night and day become one. For three to four hours we drive out on the ice by snow machine to fish. I love to put my line through the ice into the cold clear water to catch the great Arctic Char. Most will eat the delicate flesh raw and drink tea. At night I like to sleep in the canvas tent.

Kenojuak Ashevak cc

ARTIST

INTERLUNAR

We have come TO THE EDGE:

the lake gives off its hush;

in the outer night there is a barred owl

calling, like a moth

against the ear, from the far shore

which is invisible.

The lake, vast and dimensionless,

doubles everything, the stars,

the boulders, itself, even the darkness

that you can walk so long in

it becomes light.

Margaret Atwood cc
AUTHOR

Canada creates awe. OUR LAND IS SO VAST, SO SILENT AND SO COMPELLING THAT it inspires an appropriate measure of humility and proportion. To gaze on the fjord of Gros Morne, the silhouette of Percé Rock, the tumult of Niagara Falls or the ageless calm of the rain forest in the Queen Charlotte Islands, is to understand that each of us is part of a great chain of being that stretches back to time immemorial. We are part of a continuum of generations past and generations yet unborn. I never feel this more than when I am in my native Manitoba, looking at the reflections of the stars as they shine on the midnight stillness of Lake Winnipeg. At moments like this, envy, ambition and daily woes are forgotten. Like the ancients, we marvel in God's bounty and know that life is good.

Thomas S. Axworthy OC
EXECUTIVE DIRECTOR, HISTORICA FOUNDATION OF CANADA

There is magic in a reflection. I KNOW OF NO ONE WHO IS LEFT UNMOVED

by the image of a piece of nature repeated below in still water.

To glide silently in a canoe along a rocky, forested shoreline

across a perfect reflection is to be suspended in a world

that can only be described as heavenly.

Robert Bateman OC

ARTIST

When I think of Canada, TWO IMAGES REMAIN VIVIDLY IN MY MEMORY.

The first goes back to about 1925 when we lived near Burnaby, British Columbia.

My good friend Barbara and I used to walk together regularly. One morning

in early winter we came upon a tiny field mouse, frozen and dead, on some

raised ice crystals. This delicate corpse was a reminder that the country

and the climate can occasionally wear a cold mantle of cruelty.

Many years later, when we first came to New Brunswick,

a friend showed us a deep green mossy bank in a nearby

valley where pure orange chanterelles grew in late July. I'll

never forget the striking image of the orange mushrooms

amidst the deep green moss. Nor my new awareness of

the gentleness and beauty in the land we call home.

Canada is an endless place of discovery, as is each of our lives.

Molly Bobak CM

ARTIST

Jack pines stand SILHOUETTED AGAINST A CRIMSON SKY, THEIR TWISTED SHAPES BIRTHED impossibly in pink rock crevasses as old as time. A loon call pierces silent mists, hanging over the glass-still lake. The smell of the earth is sweet, after a spectacular thunderstorm, a symphony of flashing lights and deepest thunder in which each crack seemed to rend the world apart. An elegant procession of deer march inexorably across the frozen lake so close you can almost touch them. This intoxicating landscape, everchanging, beckoning, draws me like a desired *bien aimée.* Its ferocity and deceptive calm puts me in touch with my inner music.

Boris Brott oc

ARTISTIC DIRECTOR, SYMPHONY CONDUCTOR

35

It is a conviction THAT GREW IN ME OVER THE YEARS. I SHARED A REMARKABLE childhood living beside one of the world's great Rivers with other children who came from Aboriginal and Asian cultural roots. The Skeena River, "K'Sh'ian" or the River of Mists in northwestern British Columbia, forms the current of my personal landscape, but any River can be a catalyst for dreams. Sustained by the bountiful Pacific Ocean and a wondrous temperate rain forest that harbours us all here still, the first peoples of this land have lived along this coast and on these great Rivers since "the beginning of time." Many different indigenous nations founded their societies, cultures, languages and systems of government here and, over eons of time, became as "one" with their environment. What is perhaps surprising now, is that those of us who arrived later are increasingly aware of the "tugs and pulls" of the natural world that surrounds us in such abundance. Most of us are ever more conscious that the land we live with is inevitably coaxing us into its own image, just as it did all those generations who preceded us in this unmatched and magnificent land.

The Hon. Iona V. Campagnolo PC, CM, OBC
LIEUTENANT-GOVERNOR OF BRITISH COLUMBIA

My HIDING PLACE

Naked among trees, lost,

Staring out to sea.

Maury Chaykin ACTOR

Water DEFINES OUR NATION

as much as it defines island nations like England

and Japan, or dyked lands such as Holland. Water

scours and pummels and licks and crushes and

floods and buries Canada, and has done so for

billions of years.

In Canada, when we speak of water, we're speaking of ourselves. Canadians are known to be unextravagant, and one explanation of this might be that we know that wasted water means a diminished collective soul; polluted waters mean a sickened soul. Water is the basis of our self-identity, and when we dream of canoes and thunderstorms and streams and even snowballs, we're dreaming about our innermost selves.

Douglas Coupland AUTHOR, VISUAL ARTIST

My heritage in Canada REACHES BACK TO SAULT STE. MARIE well before Confederation. This gives me a great sense of awareness and appreciation for my northern Ontario roots.

Northern Ontario is a powerful experience, tempered only by the seasons. It challenges one's fortitude with an amazingly rugged terrain, just as it rewards those who embrace its remote beauty.

I have no doubt that each geographic region of Canada offers unique influences to its people. At the same time, I believe that each region reflects a parallel to that of northern Ontario, in that its people most often find themselves far from each other while still remaining a community at large, united in spirit and dedicated to the land.

Ken Danby CM

ARTIST

Watching the great Atlantic Ocean CRASHING AGAINST

the black ancient rocks, one is frozen in a moment so exquisite, unable to speak

or think—surrounded in light—hope.

Shirley Douglas ACTOR; SPOKESPERSON, CANADIAN HEALTH COALITION

Of all the images of Canada held in my mind, NONE IS MORE VIVID AND MORE precious to me than the pre-dawn radiance of Northern Lights over Manitoulin Island.

It happened almost fifty years ago; I had not seen Northern Lights before, when one August weekend, my husband and I were camping on the island and needed to get up very early in order to catch the ferry at Tobermory.

We got up before sunrise, yet there was light, though without shadows. The heavens seemed to sparkle and glisten, with streaking hues appearing and fading. The grass and the shrubs seemed to be of a different colour and texture than the night before.

We stood in awe, feeling as if we were witness to creation itself.

We knew then that we had received a gift that would be forever with us.

Ursula M. Franklin CC, OONT, FRSC

UNIVERSITY PROFESSOR EMERITA, UNIVERSITY OF TORONTO

47

Nestled at the foot of the Pembina Hills IN THE FERTILE PRAIRIE PLAINS

is my hometown, Morden. It is

surrounded by some of the most

productive farmland in Canada,

with vast flat expanses of yellow wheat

or sunflowers eddying to and fro

in the breeze, ready to be harvested.

The protein-rich kernels of wheat

are destined to fill prairie elevators

silhouetted against the azure sky,

punctuated by billowing white clouds,

floating by like white cotton balls blown

along by a gentle western breeze.

As Robert Browning wrote: "God's in

His heaven—All's right with the world!"

Henry Friesen CC, MD, FRSC
DISTINGUISHED PROFESSOR EMERITUS, UNIVERSITY OF MANITOBA

I swam around an island once. AN ISLAND IN A LAKE

on an island in the ocean. I stayed close to the shore of the small island

and drank the water as I circumnavigated. I was alone. A dragonfly my only escort.

Vicki Gabereau BROADCASTER

I am always struck BY JUST HOW MANY MOUNTAINS AND GLACIERS
there are in Canada. Most humans live only in the valleys but the remote
backcountry is enticing to us skiers. We dream of laying down tracks. First, long
slow ones as we climb up with ever-changing vistas. The view from the top is
definitely part of the reward—

but nothing can match the

feeling of freedom and the

pleasure of skiing untracked

powder as you make your way

back down.

Nancy Greene Raine oc
OLYMPIC GOLD AND SILVER MEDALLIST, SKIING

Of all the bottomless wonders THIS GREAT LAND HOLDS,

none draws me more insistently than the harshly mysterious and

relentlessly beautiful Badlands of southern Alberta. Home now to the

hardiest of creatures, it is also the burial ground of the dinosaurs. To stand

under a dome of stars, guarded by hoodoos, and know that within a step

in any direction lies the bone of an animal that lived some 75 million

years ago—well, then I know my place in the world.

Paul Gross ACTOR, WRITER, DIRECTOR

Experience and imagination HAVE MERGED; THE TWO NORTHS have become one. And that one is the land itself, with all its stretching, untrammeled, awesome beauty, a land like no other place on earth, that is ours, that shapes us and defines us and makes us who we are. So that to go there, even for the first time, is also to go home.

Peter Gzowski CC

BROADCASTER, AUTHOR

Growing up on the West Coast, MY FIRST MEMORIES AS A CHILD are of the ocean, rivers and lakes of British Columbia. When I wheeled across Canada at the end of the Man In Motion World Tour, I came to realize that our waterways are the lifeblood of our country and distinguish Canada in the world community. It is our responsibility to protect the quality and integrity of our water for future generations.

Rick Hansen cc

PRESIDENT AND CEO, RICK HANSEN INSTITUTE

The natural beauty of Canada STILL EVOKES

the same sense of wonder I felt upon arriving in my adopted

homeland 50 years ago. This feeling is renewed whenever I glimpse the

rugged shores of Newfoundland, the expansive lacework of colourful lakes

and islands dotting Canada's interior and the majesty of the Canadian

Rockies, or marvel at the images of the untouched splendour of our

Arctic landscape.

M. Daria Haust MD, FRCPC

PROFESSOR EMERITUS OF PATHOLOGY, UNIVERSITY OF WESTERN ONTARIO

Long long before THE EUROPEANS CAME TO NORTH AMERICA, before Stonehenge or the Pyramids were built nine thousand years ago, communities existed in this severe, often foreboding but exceedingly beautiful land we now call Newfoundland and Labrador.

The Hon. Max House CM, MD, LLD, FRCPC
LIEUTENANT-GOVERNOR OF NEWFOUNDLAND AND LABRADOR

In the afterglow of sunset, THE LAKE SURFACE now perfectly reflects the sky, so that inverting the image of sky, treeline and water would produce exactly the same picture.

Reflections hang there silently before me like a surreal painting— earthbound lake and land, made possible by their heavenly context. I'm reminded of Shakespeare's play within a play, or dream within a dream. Which is real? Which is reflected? Which is Heaven, which is Earth?

If there is a Heaven, then it is here on Earth simply waiting to be noticed. Life could not have been breathed into anything more beautiful.

Monte Hummel oc

AUTHOR; PRESIDENT, WORLD WILDLIFE FUND CANADA

I lay my body TO THE GROUND, WHISPER MY GRATITUDE

The joy in spirit, in all of my senses a good mood.

Rita Joe CM

POET

For his 80th birthday MY FATHER WANTED TO GO WHITE-WATER RAFTING

in the Yukon. Despite some initial trepidation on my part we set out with

some friends to experience twelve days in the great Canadian wilderness.

Earlier trips together had included the spirituality and peace of the

Queen Charlotte Islands and the wild beauty of southeastern Alaska.

Although I was cold and wet most of my time in the Yukon,

we had an amazing adventure. The majesty of the mountains and

the cold rushing water of the Tatshenshini River were constant reminders

of the amazing beauty and power of Mother Nature.

Karen Kain CC

PRINCIPAL DANCER, NATIONAL BALLET OF CANADA, 1970–97

I am spiritually connected TO THE WATER.

For ten years I spent six hours a day rowing back and forth on Elk Lake in Victoria.

I know every sound and smell of this lake. I know which way the wind is blowing and the

likelihood of a storm blowing in. I know where the bald eagles and grey herons will be

perching. The coots always warn me of hitting a buoy by obligingly sitting on the precise

ones I can't see clearly from a distance. I know how the water moves with different winds.

Yes, it is especially the water that I know.

Sometimes, ever so unexpectedly, on a day when the sun

is out and the water is flat, I touch magic. The water is

transformed; in spots it is deeper and gentler than ever

before, and my boat and my body arc in complete

harmony with the water's movement. We are carried

along as one. I don't want to breathe; I don't want to do

anything intentional for fear of shattering this moment.

For a moment I know magic.

Silken Laumann THREE-TIME OLYMPIC MEDALLIST, ROWING

Cape Breton Island IS WHERE CULTURE, NATURE AND PEOPLE ARE EXTENSIONS OF ONE ANOTHER.

The traditional music is alive and vibrant with an energy and a pulse that reaches right into your soul and stays there long after the fiddler has finished playing.

The scenery has a quiet power that will open the eyes of your heart through the peace of the forest, the strength of the hills and the dance of the ocean.

The people are warm and inviting, full of character and charm, with a joyful spirit that flows from their very core.

Yet, Cape Breton's most beautiful quality is what she gives to her people: a peace and confidence, a sense of pride and joy that fills you with a deep, honest appreciation for life. What Cape Breton gives, you keep forever.

Natalie MacMaster ENTERTAINER

Being born in Timmins, Ontario, I FELT A CONNECTION

to the water, rock and trees, particularly when the water turned to ice—

that was the essential ingredient that influenced my life.

Senator Frank Mahovlich CM

HOCKEY HALL OF FAME

To get my boat FROM ONE SIDE OF THE COUNTRY TO THE OTHER

I have driven from my home in Toronto to Victoria over and over.

Much to everyone's surprise I love the drive: four days of

completely new experiences, weather systems and changing

vistas every few hours. Precambrian rocks, pines, birch; yellow prairie

fields with only slightly rolling horizons; the badlands with its striated

valleys; and the two mountain ranges with their distinctly

different peaks, one dramatic and sharp, the other majestic and worn.

On each drive, as a rower I can't help but marvel at the water. Each

river and lake that I pass—whether it is the lakes of Muskoka, Huron

or Superior; the rivers of the Prairies; the lakes of British Columbia's

interior or the coastal bays in Victoria—invites me with its brilliance to

come and play to get off the road and go for a sweet silent row and

enjoy its view.

Marnie McBean THREE-TIME OLYMPIC GOLD MEDALLIST, ROWING

I had flown AN OLD CESSNA FLOATPLANE AROUND
Canada making a TV show, but coming to Bathurst Inlet was the
crowning of a great adventure.

I walked up a ridge. At its crest, I could see for maybe 80 kilometres. I sat down on the spongy tundra plants
to rest, marvelling that, at my feet, there was a riot of colours, yet even a short distance away the colours
became a subdued palate of browns, grays and ochres. It was silent except for the rustling of the wind.
I could hear the blood moving about my body with my heartbeat. My breathing was deafening. In my
ears I could hear a high-pitched whine, a gift from the din of civilization.

I fell asleep. When I awoke I sat up, breathed deeply and looked
again at my surroundings.

I had the curious feeling that everything was revolving around this
spot. I was completely alone.

But I wasn't lonely.

Murray McLauchlan CM
SINGER/SONGWRITER, AUTHOR, BROADCASTER

Canoeing in Algonquin Park, MAKING ANGELS IN THE SNOW, partaking in the cottage-country exodus from the cities are experiences I haven't had the benefit of being a part of. As an immigrant from India, now living in downtown Toronto, Canada's natural vistas are in my peripheral vision rather than in direct sight or ethos. However, just beyond metro's skyscrapers is the Canadian sky. A sky so breathtaking in its blueness, so pristine in its clarity, so infinite in its potential that it fills me with nothing other than awe. Being enveloped within this sky is a uniquely Canadian experience. An experience that reflects Canada's ability to shelter its disparate strands under a unifying azure umbrella.

Deepa Mehta FILMMAKER, WRITER

DIFFERENT AND ONE

When EARTH AND SKY

Converge

An ancient union recurs

Reminding

Difference is not separate

The earth and sky

Teach

Inspiring our souls

Reminding

Difference is beauty

When earth and sky

Merge

Both retaining their beauty

Reminding

We are different and one.

Ovide Mercredi CHIEF OF THE ASSEMBLY OF FIRST NATIONS, 1991–97

I was doing a tour OF A CHILDREN'S PLAY ON RACISM,

and the last stop was the Queen Charlotte Islands. We were invited to

lunch at someone's place on one of the little islands. So we kayaked over

and after lunch I went out by myself. Before I became an actor I had

entertained thoughts of becoming a marine biologist. The ocean has

always been quite soothing to me. Anyway about 100 yards ahead of me

were three whales sunning themselves, I guess. It really was an incredible

moment. However I did get nervous and slowly made my way back

to the island.

Colin Mochrie COMEDIAN, ACTOR, WRITER

The ocean, RED SOIL, SALT AIR, BEAUTIFUL SUNSETS,

warm and friendly people and the laid-back lifestyle make

Nova Scotia a constant lure for me. There I feel safe and serene.

It is my light at the end of the tunnel.

Anne Murray cc

ENTERTAINER

The Haliburton Highlands ARE TO ME AN INTRINSIC PART OF CANADA.

Its beauty, to my way of thinking, is unparalleled elsewhere in the world.

Oscar Peterson CC

JAZZ MUSICIAN, COMPOSER, AUTHOR

I love the land BECAUSE IT LOVES ME BACK THROUGH ITS NATURAL CHARACTER;

I know it has taught me, nourished me and inspired me; ever life-giving, ever distinctive;

telling me who and what I am, and why I live here.

Gordon Pinsent cc

ACTOR, DIRECTOR, WRITER

I have always loved VAST OPEN SPACES.

For me there is something liberating about them: enabling the imagination

to roam freely, encouraging bold thoughts, expanding the mind and lifting

the spirit. As a zoologist I enjoy seeing animals in their natural habitats.

Imagine then my delight when I visited Wapusk National Park. I was

captivated by unending vistas of ice, swirling patterned ice, and snow.

I was enchanted by polar bears strolling and cavorting while dwarfed by the

immenseness of their environment.

A memory I shall cherish forever.

Betty Roots PHD, DSC, FRSC
PROFESSOR EMERITUS, UNIVERSITY OF TORONTO

When stresses pile up, I FIND that a mental picture of the Lake Huron waterside just before sunset is a reliable source of inner peace. It seems to me that a love of water, be it in our lakes, rivers or oceans, is a fundamental part of what it means to feel Canadian.

Stuart L. Smith MD; CHAIR, NATIONAL ROUNDTABLE ON THE ENVIRONMENT AND THE ECONOMY

It was in "the bush" THAT I CREATED MY OWN WORLD AS A CHILD.

Trees moaning and creaking in the wind, exquisite jewel-like flowers, hilarious puffballs,

noisy woodpeckers, garter snakes rustling through leaves and ancient rocks to lie on.

There, I was protected from the adult world, inspired by the power and mystery of the forest.

Anything was possible.

Sonia Smits ACTOR

Travel a thousand miles BY TRAIN AND YOU ARE A BRUTE;

pedal five hundred on a bicycle and you remain basically a bourgeois;

paddle a hundred in a canoe and you are already a child of nature.

The Rt. Hon. Pierre Elliott Trudeau cc

PRIME MINISTER 1968–79, 1979–84

On the canvas OF THE PRAIRIE SKY,

young boys and girls can imagine and sketch a future. You can see possibilities and places yet to be

discovered. You can ask how far is far and know that it's within your reach. The endless blue beckons you.

Even a menacing storm approaching causes no fear, because you can confront it, see it and prepare for it.

Pamela Wallin BROADCASTER, AUTHOR,
CANADA'S CONSUL GENERAL TO NEW YORK

This beautiful, TERRIBLE PLACE OF EXTREMES AND EXCESSES,

the ice, the rain, the wind, fierce enough to rip the features right off your face,

the constant sea changes, the horizontal snowfalls, the soft shroud of endless fog.

Newfoundland's monstrously beautiful geography, her savagely friendly people

conspire to lift you up in a ferocious embrace and never let you go.

Mary Walsh CM

WRITER, ACTOR

ACKNOWLEDGEMENTS

The desire TO SHARE THOUGHTS AND STORIES THROUGH WORDS AND PHOTOGRAPHS IS COMPELLING.
I will always be thankful to my parents, Mildred and Ed, who taught my sister, Barbara, and me about the
great outdoors as explorers would, full of curiosity and wonder. They also gave us our first cameras,
encouraging us to record the world around us. As an adult, I photographed planet Earth from space, and
from the ground I continue to capture its landscapes through my lens.

When Scott McIntyre approached me to assemble a book that would speak to our love of Canada,
I realized that the lives of many highly respected Canadians have also been touched by the diversity of our
natural world. I thank the gracious people who generously gave a personal account of an event in their lives
or a place in their hearts, or who gave their hearts in words—in spite of busy schedules. Without hesitation,
and given only the promise that their words would be associated with a photograph that I had taken of
Canada, the following Canadians responded openly to my request: Bryan Adams, Michael Adams, Susan
Aglukark, Louise Arbour, Kenojuak Ashevak, Margaret Atwood, Tom Axworthy, Robert Bateman, Molly
Bobak, Boris Brott, Iona Campagnolo, Maury Chaykin, Douglas Coupland, Ken Danby, Shirley Douglas, Ursula
Franklin, Henry Friesen, Vicki Gabereau, Nancy Greene Raine, Paul Gross, Peter Gzowski, Rick Hansen,

Daria Haust, Max House, Monte Hummel, Rita Joe, Karen Kain, Silken Laumann, Natalie MacMaster, Frank Mahovlich, Marnie McBean, Murray McLauchlan, Deepa Mehta, Ovide Mercredi, Colin Mochrie, Anne Murray, Oscar Peterson, Gordon Pinsent, Betty Roots, Stuart Smith, Sonja Smits, Pierre Elliott Trudeau, Pamela Wallin, Mary Walsh.

My gratitude extends to Christine Yankou, the editor of this book of dreams and Canadian patriotism, for her spirit and her professionalism. She believes in and is committed to Canada, actual and potential. Her sense of humour kept everyone excited and positive through the long distances and time zones. Her colleague, Calvin McLauchlan, reviewed the manuscript and kept a sharp eye on the sense of the quotes.

Parks Canada has always supported artists in expressing the beauty of the land so that others will come and be refreshed in our protected sanctuaries. Tom Lee and Bruce Amos continue their commitment, and I thank them and the fine Parks Canada wardens and interpreters who assisted me in the field.

The following individuals provided superb technical advice and support: Mary Mulder, National Sales Manager, Nikon Canada Inc., for the use of the D1X; Michael Boylan, Professional Products Manager, Kindermann (Canada) Inc; Jack Arno, Vice President Sales and Marketing; and Joe Vieira, Hasselblad Technician, Lisle-Kelco Limited.

Scott McIntyre, of Douglas & McIntyre, remained steadfast in his support of this book through a difficult period in the history of Canadian publishing. I thank him and Lucy Kenward, production editor, and Val Speidel, designer.

Thank you, Canada.

LIST OF CONTRIBUTORS

The type used in this book is Cartier Book. Originally created by lettering artist Carl Dair in 1966, Cartier was Canada's first typeface. In 2000, Toronto-based typographer Rod McDonald reworked the original design, creating this new typeface, Cartier Book. It is now considered a Canadian classic.